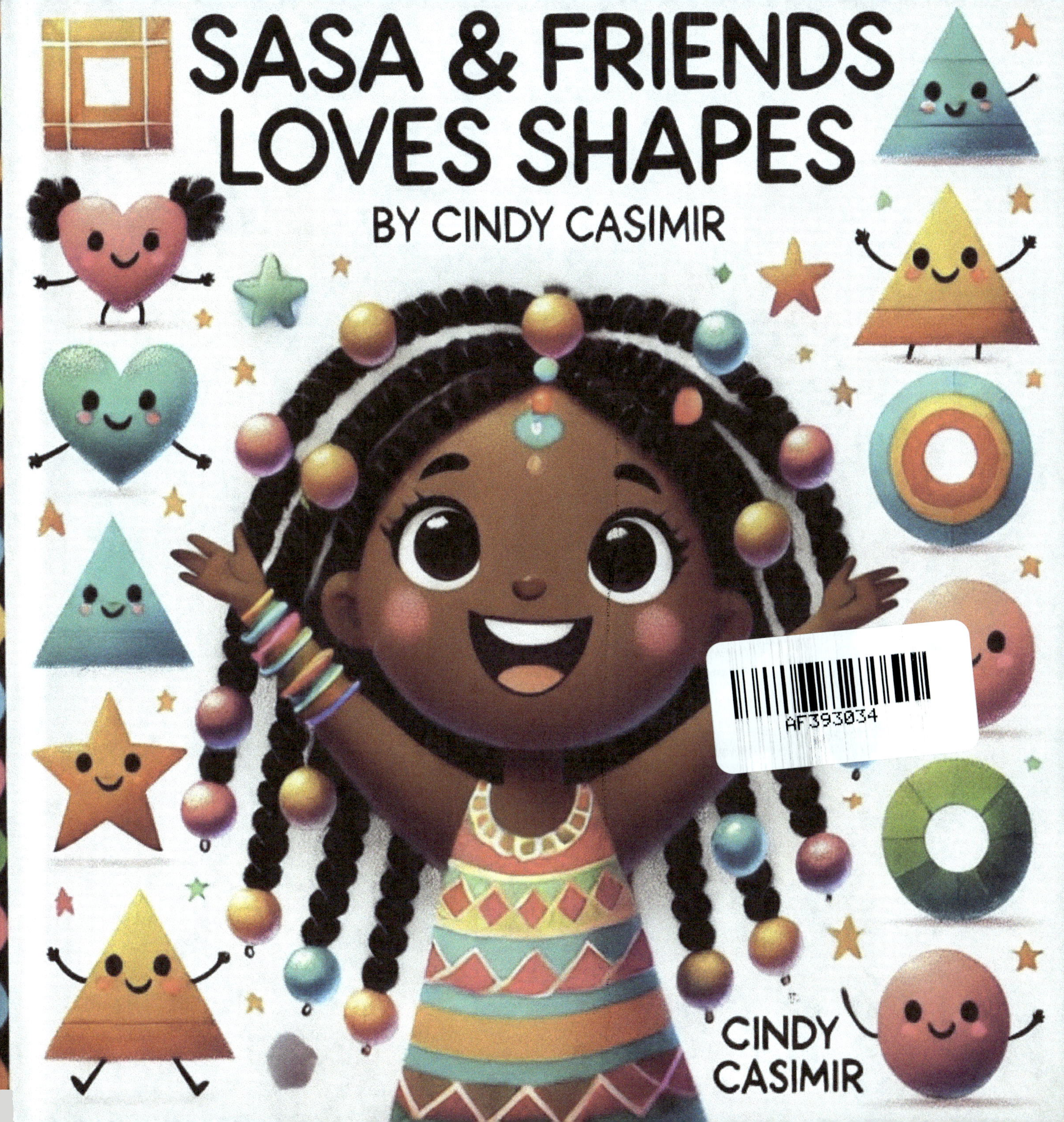

SASA & FRIENDS LOVES SHAPES

BY CINDY CASIMIR

Sasa looked up at the bright, happy sun in the sky.
"The sun is a big, round circle!" she said with a smile.
"Circles have no sides, they just go round and round!"

Cece watched her brother fly the colorful kite high in the sky.
"Kites are shaped like diamonds!" she said, smiling.
"How many sides do you see?"

Abby found a big, red block.
"This block is shaped like a square!" she said.
"Sqaures have four sides, can you count them with me?"

Maya stacked her colorful blocks one by one.
"Blocks are shaped like rectangles!" she giggled, holding one up.
"Rectangles have two long sides and two short sides."

Sara drew a big, bright heart!
"Hearts are my favorite shape," she said with a big smile.
"Can you find more shapes?"

Lulu smiled at her sandwich.
"Look, my sandwich is shaped like a triangle!"
she said excitedly.
"Triangles have three sides, can you count them?"

The stars twinkled brightly in the night sky.
“That’s my favorite shape!” said Sasa, pointing up.
“Stars shine and sparkle, what’s your favorite shape?”

Thank-you
read again

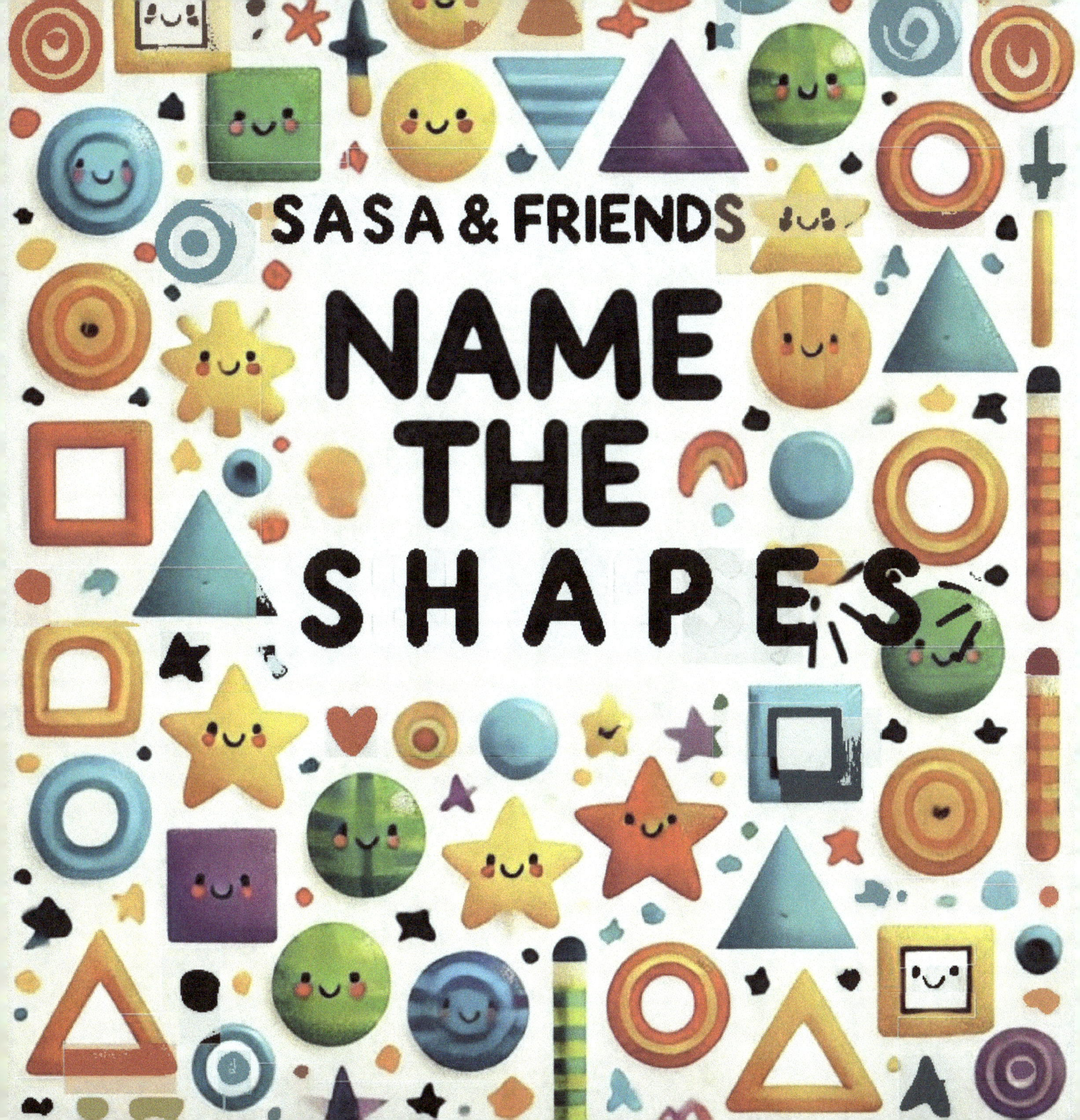

SASA & FRIENDS
NAME THE SHAPES